Ping Pong Panda

Written by
Jill Atkins

Illustrated by
Andy Hamilton

Ping Pong was a panda.

He was good at ping pong.
He was the ping pong champ.

"I have such a good green bat," he said. "With that bat, I will win."

He held his bat up high for his fans to see.

"You are the best!" they said to him.

"This is my best bat," said Ping Pong Panda.

"It will help me hit high. It will help me hit hard."

Ping Pong Panda was quick and light on his feet.

He was good at darting in and out.

He was good at winning.

"You are the best at ping pong!" said his fans.

But the next morning, when Ping Pong Panda got up, he was upset.

He had lost his best ping pong bat!

"This is not good!" he said.
"I have six bats, but that one was the best."

Ping Pong Panda needed that bat to win.

"Look in this chest," said his chum, Pong Ping.

But the bat was not in the chest.

"Look under this chair," said Pong Ping.

But the bat was not under the chair.

"What am I going to do?" said Ping Pong Panda.

Now Ping Pong Panda did not win at ping pong.

With no green bat, he felt lost.

"This is such a shock!" he said.
"What am I going to do?"

He ran into his garden.

A frog was sitting on a green pad in the pond.

"Wait! That is not a pad!" said Ping Pong with a big grin. "That is my best green bat!"

The frog hopped off.

Ping Pong Panda looked at his bat. "Now I can start winning," he said.

And so he did!